# Thailand-Burma Border: History and Current Issues

Ariana Zarleen

February 2015

First Printing: 2015

ISBN 978-952-68283-0-5

Author: Ariana Zarleen

Cover design by: Saara Holmas

Publisher: Burma Link

This book has been edited from information collected by Burma Link, a legally registered non-profit organisation that spreads awareness of the ongoing struggle of Burma's ethnic nationalities and displaced people, and shares their voices and stories with the world.

For more information, please visit Burma Link's website at www.burmalink.org

All proceeds from book sales go to support Burma Link's work on the Thailand-Burma border.

## CONTENTS

## Overview of Thailand-Burma Border

Burma has experienced one of the biggest humanitarian crisis and most protracted refugee situations in the world. Millions of people from Burma, mostly ethnic nationalities in the country's borderlands, have fled armed conflicts and Burmese military run human rights abuses that have spanned over several decades. The civil war that started with the Karen armed opposition in 1949 has been dubbed as the longest ongoing internal conflict in the world, and the Burmese military, in order to defeat ethnic armed opposition, has targeted their military campaigns against ethnic civilians. The result has been ongoing persecution of ethnic villagers particularly in rural areas where ethnic armed opposition has been operating.

In total, around three million people are thought to have fled armed conflicts in Burma (Refugees International, 2014), whilst more than half a million remain internally displaced (IDMC, 2014). Due to the close proximity, hundreds of thousands have fled conflict and persecution in eastern Burma to neighbouring Thailand. Most of these refugees are Karen, Karenni, Shan, and Mon. There are also refugees from Burma who belong to Arakanese, Chin, Rohingya, Kachin, Naga and countless of other ethnic nationalities. As the government has exerted repressive military control over the resource rich ethnic borderlands all over the country, ethnic armies have fought to protect their lands and their people, and ethnic civilians have suffered the consequences. In addition, thousands of majority Burman (also called Bamar) civilians, usually due to their involvement in the political pro-democracy struggle in Rangoon or in other major cities, have crossed the border to flee from the repressive government.

Meanwhile, as the military control in Burma has gradually eroded livelihoods and induced poverty through forced labour, arbitrary taxation, and restrictions on movement and trade, many civilians have fled to Thailand simply to avoid further impoverishment (KHRG, 2008). Others have come with the hope of accessing education, medicine, or work opportunities. Distinguishing between refugees and migrants is difficult in this context; thousands of students, for example, have entered the refugee camps solely for education while thousands of *de facto*[1] refugees reside outside the camps as undocumented immigrants. With the Thai authorities placing significant restrictions on the lives of refugees and the work of the United Nations High Commissioner for Refugees (UNHCR) in the refugee camps, many refugees warranting international protection have chosen to live illegally outside of the camps. At the same time, those who have fled military-induced poverty, for example, are not recognised as refugees under international law.

**Young boy in Mae La refugee camp, the largest of the camps in in Thailand with over 40,000 residents. (Photo: Feliz Solomon)**

No one knows the exact numbers of those who have crossed the border from Burma to Thailand, and much less the number of people who would fall under international protection as refugees. The statistics put together by the UNHCR and The Border Consortium (TBC), the latter an aid coordination network on the border, are gross understatements of the real refugee figures as countless of de facto refugees remain outside of their protection and aid. According to the UNHCR's figures from January 2015, Thailand hosts 72,900 registered refugees and 51,500 "people in refugee-like situations" from Burma

[1] Factual refugees who fall under The 1951 United Nations Convention's international definition of a refugee.

(UNHCR, 2015a). According to TBC figures from December 2014, a total of 110,607 refugees reside in ten refugee camps along the Thailand-Burma border (TBC, December, 2014). TBC's database includes all registered and unregistered refugees who reside in the camps. As for the internally displaced persons (IDPs), Internal Displacement Monitoring Centre (IDMC) estimates that there were 643,000 IDPs due to conflict and violence in Burma as of July 2014, majority of them in southeast Burma (IDMC, 2014).

*"It is better to run away. If they [the SPDC] catch us they will be very mean to us, it is better to escape. It is better to live in Thailand, if you live in Burma now it is very, very bad." (Naw M–, a 23-year-old female from K— village, Papun District, interviewed in February 2007; KHRG, 2008, p. 135)*

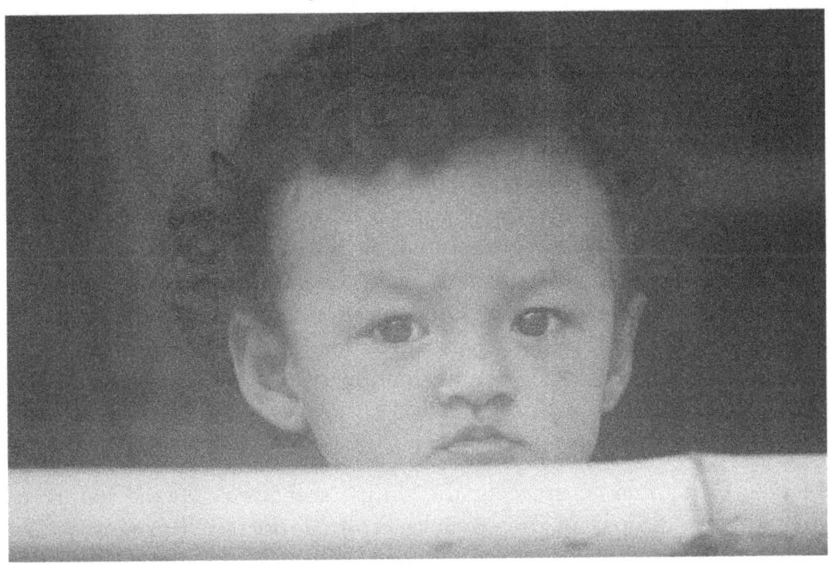

**A young boy in a hiding site in Lu Thaw Township, Papun District, in May 2010. (Photo: KHRG)**

The thousands of refugees in the Thailand-Burma border camps have lived in a protracted situation for years, even decades, with no way out. Their prolonged confinement in the camps has created not only many protection concerns but also social and psychological problems. As the Thai authorities have prohibited refugees from travelling, farming, or collecting firewood outside the camps, the refugees' coping mechanisms have been severely eroded. Despite Burma's opening up in recent years, TBC reports that very few people have spontaneously returned home (TBC, 2014a). This observation is even more significant considering that life in the refugee camps has recently become more difficult and uncertain than ever; there are ongoing significant reductions in aid and food rations given to refugees because international aid has shifted from the border to central Burma; rumours of forced repatriation have begun spreading across refugee communities; and increasing travel and living restrictions in the camps have made refugees' lives even more constrained since the Thai military coup in May 2014 (see e.g. Saw Yan Naing, July, 2014a).

Inside the Karen State in eastern Burma, it is easy to see why thousands cross the border to Thailand to escape impoverishment. In 2010, TBC completed a food security and poverty assessment in the area and reported that over two-thirds of households were not able to meet their basic needs (TBC, 2011). In 2012, TBC found that 59% of people on rural southeast Burma were impoverished and 73% lacked access to safe drinking water (TBC, 2012b). Another TBC survey conducted during March and April 2013 (TBC, 2013c) found similar results. These statistics are particularly troubling considering that Burma is a resource rich country where the standard of living for the population should be considerably higher than this. Through economic mismanagement (or deliberate concentration of wealth in the hands of Burmese generals) and military terrorisation of the civilian population, Burma had been transformed from one of the wealthiest Southeast Asian countries to becoming one of the world's least developed countries in 1987 (Booth, 2003).

Due to difficulties in entering the camps and the restricted nature of life in the camps, an overwhelming majority of Burma's exiles, including de facto refugees, live in Thailand as illegal aliens. For generations, they have lived under constant fear of deportation and abuse, trying to build their lives in the peripheries of Thai society, often working in unsafe conditions, underpaid and at risk of exploitation and human trafficking (Green-Rauenhorst et al., 2008). Meanwhile, thousands of refugees have died in the border camps never able to return to their homeland. And all the while, a new generation of refugees has been born in the camps, many of whom have never left the gates of the only home they know.

Annually, the UN has passed resolutions that call on the Burmese government to respect human rights (e.g. UN General Assembly, 2014a), which has meant little to the millions of people who have spent so much of their lives in a limbo—not to mention the hundreds of thousands of others who remain displaced inside Burma and elsewhere outside the country's borders.

Although there is a framework of international principles that recognise and protect the inherent dignity and equal, inalienable rights of humanity, these principals have little significance to refugees from Burma who live in Thailand. According to Article 14 (1) of the Universal Declaration of Human Rights (UDHR); "Everyone has the right to seek and to enjoy in other countries asylum from persecution." The 1951 United Nations Convention and its 1967 Protocol Relating to the Status of Refugees include the principle of non-refoulement; "No Contracting State shall expel or return a refugee in any manner whatsoever to the frontiers of territories where his life or freedom would be threatened on account of his race, religion, nationality, membership of a particular social group or political opinion." Thailand is not a party to the 1951 Convention or its 1967 Protocol.

**Migrants looking for recyclable plastic in the Mae Sot rubbish dump (Photo: Burma Link)**

On the other side of the coin, one must acknowledge the immense difficulty in dealing with a refugee situation as vast and protracted as the one along the Thailand-Burma border. Accordingly, in 2008, the International Rescue Committee (IRC) pleaded the international community to increase support for essential services to unrecognised refugees. The IRC stated that the Thai government should not have to shoulder the responsibility of hosting the refugee population on their own (Green-Rauenhorst, Jacobsen, & Pyne, 2008).

As Thailand has been a host to scores of exiles from Burma for decades, it has also become a vibrant hub for Burma's opposition and capacity building movement. The border is home to numerous local and international aid, education, advocacy, and pro-democracy organisations that have been based in Thailand for decades, working in exile towards peaceful and free Burma through capacity building programmes and running awareness raising trainings and workshops, as well as documenting human rights abuses inside Burma. Due to this, a high percentage of the people of Burma who have been educated in human rights and Burma issues, among other fields of study, live on the Thailand-Burma border. Their knowledge and skills will be invaluable for the future of Burma, especially when building a solid foundation of institutions that will be integral to a functioning civil society based on principles of freedom and justice.

A number of local and international community-based organisations (CBOs) and non-governmental organisations (NGOs) in Thailand also provide aid for IDPs in eastern Burma who cannot be reached from inside the country. With non-existing health facilities in many rural areas, thousands of people annually also travel across the border to receive medical treatment at the Mae Tao Clinic in the Thai border town of Mae Sot in Thailand's Tak Province. The clinic has treated hundreds of thousands of patients from Burma for free for over two decades.

Although the government has recently made changes to bring the country closer to a democracy, the effects of these initiatives have yet to reach the country's ethnic border areas. And while there is now less fighting and direct attacks on civilians in eastern Burma, land grabbing has increased and Burma Army is fortifying their positions in ethnic areas (see e.g. KHRG, 2013, 2014), bringing to question their commitment to peace. For many people and organisations along the

Thailand-Burma border, the main change that occurred as a result of the reforms has been a significant reduction in aid and funding. While local organisations now have more opportunities to work inside Burma, many CBOs are concerned that donors are pushing them inside the country before they feel ready to safely operate there. Even when some organisations feel relatively safe to operate inside, many of their programmes such as capacity building internships, that in Thailand would have access to foreign volunteers, internet, electricity and critical information, are severely hampered when forced to be conducted inside. Other times the organisations, when pushed inside, have to make numerous compromises to their work, including self-censoring information and language used in their publications, at times forcing the organisations to compromise the very core values and goals that they were founded on in the first place.

There are now also growing fears that refugees will be forcibly repatriated before conditions permit them to return with a sense of hope and dignity. Talks about repatriation have caused anxiety among the communities in the camps as formidable obstacles for safe repatriation, including lack of sustainable peace, ongoing human rights violations, and widespread landmine contamination, still remain.

The border has been a vibrant hub for working towards a free, democratic and free Burma for decades. Until the government of Burma shows genuine willingness of discussing the political goals of the ethnic people, it is only a matter of time before the armed conflict shifts back to southeast Burma where most of the refugees and exiles in Thailand fled from. The international community, including donors, should continue to support work on the border before and during any transition. If there really is to be real change in Burma, it is imperative that the movement on the border is fully included and supported in taking part in the process.

## History of Conflict and Flight

The plight of ethnic nationalities has been ignored by the Burmese government ever since Burma gained independence in 1948. The result has been constant war and conflict between armed ethnic opposition and the Burmese military.

The conflict started with the Karen armed struggle for equality and self-determination in 1949 and quickly spread all over the country hand in hand with the growing subjugation of ethnic areas by the government. In the 1960s, the situation went from bad to worse as Ne Win took over the government in a military coup, established an authoritarian regime, and began a massive counter-insurgency campaign "Four Cuts[2]" that targeted civilian populations in an effort to defeat the ethnic opposition armies. At the time, the Karen National Union (KNU), and its armed wing Karen National Liberation Army (KNLA), was arguably the most significant of Burma's ethnic opposition groups, controlling large areas of territory across the Karen State and its adjacent areas, including villages near Rangoon. Shan, Karenni, Mon, and other ethnic nationalities also controlled much of their traditional land along the border for decades. Eventually, a series of Burma Army attacks pushed KNU troops back towards the Thai border, and in 1984, a massive Burmese offensive in eastern Burma drove 10,000 Karen refugees into Thailand's Tak Province (see e.g. TBC, 2012a). This marked the beginning of the refugee flow from Burma into Thailand.

The government's Four Cuts policy resulted in the destruction of tens of thousands of communities, and hundreds of thousands fled, some making it all the way to Thailand. Thousands of villages, especially in the Karen and Karenni States, were burned to the ground, including houses, religious buildings, schools, belongings, and sometimes even domestic animals. In many areas, it became the norm for the villagers to live in a constant fear of the Burma Army coming to their village, terrorising the villagers, stealing their food, forcing villagers to become

[2] The Four Cuts policy aims to cut off the four main links - food, finance, intelligence and recruits - between civilians and armed opposition forces by a campaign of non-stop military harassment.

porters and mine sweepers, raping ethnic women, and torturing and killing anyone suspected of having a connection the ethnic armed opposition. Whilst some villagers endured the abuse by developing warning systems and repeatedly fleeing to the jungle, others, who had heard about Thailand, decided to leave their village for good. Others still had no choice as their village was already in ashes on the ground.

**Karen Revolution Day celebrated in a liberated area inside the Karen State on January 31, 2013. (Photo: Burma Link)**

In 1984, according to TBC (2004), the refugees and the NGOs that worked with them thought that the Burma Army would retreat after the dry season, and most refugees believed that they could return to their homeland. These hopes were soon crushed as it became clear that the Burma Army had no plans on retreating, and attacks continued.

After the 8888 uprising taking place in Burma in 1988, around 10,000 mainly Burman student activists fled government persecution to the Thailand-Burma border, and refugees realised there was no going back. Whilst being a huge blow to the refugees, this was also the first time that alliances were made between ethnic and pro-democracy movements; the Burman students were now exchanging stories with the ethnic people about their common enemy (TBC, 2004).

*"For the first time in Burma, there was a connection between the democracy issue and the ethnic issue. Before this, Ne Win had been successful in persuading people that Burma was fighting a war with insurgents who were trying to tear the country apart… The international community had pretty much accepted that version and the ethnic groups had got very little sympathy." (Jack Dunford, the Executive Director of TBC 1984-2012; TBC, 2004, p. 22)*

Burma Army attacks and associated refugee outflows continued and in 1989, a fierce attack in Karenni State drove the first large inflow of Karenni refugee across the border to Mae Hong Son Province in Thailand (TBC, 2004). Although the government signed ceasefires with several non-state armed groups in the 1990s, conflict and abuses continued and refugees kept crossing the border.

By the 1990s, the ethnic and pro-democracy organisations on the border had become a fairly united front of opposition that shared their headquarters with the KNU in Manerplaw, Karen State. Undoubtedly the biggest blow to the border groups and the KNU took place in 1995 with the fall of Manerplaw. This huge setback seemed to be a result of clever psychological warfare by the military regime. It is widely believed that the Burma Army exploited grievances among a group of Buddhist Karen, who were unhappy with the Christian KNU leadership and broke away to form the Democratic Karen Buddhist Army (DKBA). The DKBA quickly aligned with the government troops and attacked Manerplaw. These events were enormous setbacks to the whole opposition movement and significantly weakened the Karen armed resistance against the regime.

By mid-1990s, refugees in the camps began feeling increasingly unsafe, as the DKBA, supported by the Burma Army, launched several offensives to the refugee camps:

*"We used to be so scared all the time… We had a system in the night of hitting bamboo to raise the alert. You would lie awake all the time, afraid of every little sound in the dark. When we were attacked you had to run out into the dark with some food and wait in the forest until dawn." (K'Nyaw Paw, 23, then a teenager in the camp; TBC, 2004, p. 26)*

Noe Myint, a KNLA soldier, described an attack in Baw Naw camp saying that most of the 400-500 houses, including his, were burnt down by the DKBA, and one young girl died in the fire (Burma Link, 2014a). The DKBA also attacked Mae Ra Ma Luang, burning down the TBC rice store as well as 170 houses, killing one child and two adults. In 1997, the DKBA attacked Wang Kha (Huay Kaloke) camp near Mae Sot, setting fire to about 60% of the camp and forcing refugees to flee to the jungle. The same year, three people were killed and four young girls seriously injured in Mae La camp attack (TBC, 2004).

It is believed that the DKBA was not targeting civilians, most of whom were Karen, but the KNLA resistance that was operating from the camps. For the refugees, however, the attacks meant living in constant fear of soldiers of their own ethnicity, and under increasing restrictions. Following the attacks, the village-type camps were reorganised and merged into large camps that became more and more dependent on outside aid.

**Shan-Karen freedom fighter pictured in a KNLA army camp. (Photo: Burma Link)**

In 1996 and 1997 thousands of Shan were fleeing huge relocation programmes in the Shan State that were undertaken in accordance with the government's Four Cuts policy; over 300,000 people from over 1,400 villages were forced out of their homes into relocation sites (SHRF & SWAN, 2002). Shan refugees in Thailand remain in a particularly vulnerable position as they are not recognised by the Thai government. There is only one Shan refugee camp, Kuang Jor, housing about 500 people, but it is not under the protection of the UNHCR. The recognised camps had by 1997 reached a population of over 100,000, excluding the Shan and thousands of others who lived outside the camps as undocumented migrants.

In 1997, the Burma Army launched a huge dry season offensive and for the first time in history, had access to and control over the entire border region. Sadly with the help of the Karen army DKBA, ethnic nationalities no longer controlled any significant swathes of territory (TBC, 2004). Conflict and abuse continued, and by 2006, the refugee numbers in Thailand topped 150,000 (TBC, 2012a).

**View over Mae La refugee camp (Photo: Burma Link)**

New tensions ensued on the border following the government's demand, enshrined in the 2008 Constitution, that all ceasefire groups must transform into the Border Guard Force (BGF) under the command of the Burma Army – Most groups denied the call and many longstanding ceasefire agreements unravelled. Most DKBA soldiers refused to complete their transformation into BGF units and ended their 16-year ceasefire, siding with the KNU for the first time since their breakaway in 1995. Many observers were pleased to see the KNU welcome their Karen brothers back to their side to oppose the government, despite the history between the two armed groups. During 2010 and 2011, intensified fighting between the Burmese military and ethnic armed groups along the border forced an estimated 20,000 refugees into Thailand.

Fighting also broke out in other parts of the country. In March 2011, the Burma Army attacked the Shan State Army-South (SSA-S), breaking a ceasefire reached in 1989. Ensuing fighting displaced an estimated 30,000 civilians. In June 2011, war broke out between the Burmese army and Burma's second largest non-state armed group, the Kachin Independence Army (KIA), ending a ceasefire signed in 1994. Although in smaller numbers than the groups inhabiting areas near the Thai border, many ethnic Kachin have also escaped the conflict to Thailand.

In the second half of 2011, the government began negotiating new ceasefires with several armed opposition groups (see e.g. Human Rights Watch, 2012a). Initial peace agreements were signed with most of the prominent ethnic armed groups, including a historical ceasefire agreement with the KNU/KNLA. Sporadic fighting and skirmishes have, however, been reported since (e.g. Saw Yan Naing, September, 2014; Shan Herald, September, 2012; TBC, 2012a, 2013a).

After the new nominally civilian government took office in March 2011, some political developments have begun to take place in Burma. The government has been negotiating with several armed groups, there is less fighting in the Karen State and villagers can travel more freely. Nevertheless, many crucial issues remain unresolved, including lack of progress in the peace process as well as ongoing grave violations of human rights in Burma's prisons and ethnic nationality areas. Ms. Yanghee Lee, the current Special Rapporteur on the situation of human rights in Myanmar (Burma) warned in July 2014 that there are worrying signs of possible backtracking in the reform process (UN Office of the High Commissioner for Human Rights, July, 2014).

## Refugee Camps

Many people around the world take for granted the freedom to travel and freedom to work. Others have learned to take for granted that they are unable to do so. Thousands of refugees from Burma have lived confined to the camps in Thailand for 30 years. Although refugee camps are hardly natural places to live, thousands have been born in the camps and never left. For the vast majority of them, the only way of life they have ever known is one forced to be dependent on outside assistance. For many young refugees, refugee camps are where they were born and where they grew up, and the only reality they have ever seen exists within the fences of the camp.

**Thousands have been born in the camps and never seen life outside the camp fences. This photo is from the isolated Mae La Oon camp in Mae Hong Son Province, Thailand. (Photo: Ariana Zarleen)**

Meanwhile, many older people have lived in the camps for so long that they can hardly remember their homeland anymore. This is all the while the refugee camps are only considered "temporary shelters" by Thai authorities who can close down the camps whenever they decide to do so. Thailand, in recent years, has made it no secret that they want to close the camps, causing growing concerns among the refugee population who do not feel safe to return.

When the first refugees arrived in 1984, no one could have ever predicted that they would still be there 30 years on. Majority of the refugees in the camps are Karen (79.1%) or Karenni (10.3%) from eastern Burma (TBC, December, 2014), who have fled armed conflicts and/or horrendous human rights abuse and persecution by the Burmese military. The government's policy of Four Cuts, and what has been described as the slow genocide of ethnic peoples (La Guardia, June, 2005), resulted in the destruction of tens of thousands of communities and the decline of traditional cultures.

Until 1995, refugees on the border lived in village-type settlements and were allowed to travel outside the camps to find food and shelter materials. Camp life changed dramatically after the DKBA attacks; the village-type settlements were merged into large, sprawling camps that became increasingly dependent on outside aid as residents became more and more restricted on space and movement (TBC, 2004). Refugees still frequently break the rules of confinement and as a consequence, are often detained and have occasionally even been deported (e.g. SHRF & SWAN, 2002). There are also reports of refugees been found killed outside the camp fences under mysterious circumstances (see e.g. Human Rights Watch, 2012b, pp. 37-38; Poe Kwa Lay, November 2012). Refugees have no means of seeking redress; similarly to Burmese authorities in their home country, Thai officials often seem to enjoy total impunity (see Human Rights Watch, 2012b).

Throughout the 1980s, 1990s, and 2000s, more refugees kept pouring across the border to Thailand. Alongside the growing need, a humanitarian and human rights network grew along the border. One of the organisations to respond to the crisis is The Border Consortium (TBC), which remains the main agency organising food and other aid to the refugees. TBC was originally formed by TBC's former Executive Director Jack Dundorf who was among the first people to witness and respond to the urgent needs of thousands of refugees who fled to Thailand in 1984. TBC gradually evolved into a multi-membership aid organisation, and is one of the Executive Members of the Committee for Coordination of Services to Displaced Persons in Thailand

(CCSDPT) that works together with the UNHCR to coordinate all humanitarian service and protection activities in Thailand.

| Refugee camp | Camp population | Majority Ethnicity |
|---|---|---|
| Province/Camp | Total TBC verified caseload | |
| **CHIANG MAI** | | |
| Kuang Jor | 513 | Shan |
| **MAE HONG SON** | | |
| Ban Mai Nai Soi | 11,531 | Karenni |
| Ban Mae Surin | 2,724 | Karenni |
| Mae La Oon | 10,539 | Karen |
| Mae Ra Ma Luang | 12,099 | Karen |
| **TAK** | | |
| Mae La | 40,385 | Karen |
| Umpiem Mai | 12,099 | Karen |
| Nu Po | 11,399 | Karen |
| **KANCHANABURI** | | |
| Ban Don Yang | 2,972 | Karen |
| **RATCHABURI** | | |
| Tham Hin | 6,346 | Karen |
| **TOTAL** | **110,607** | Karen 79.1%<br>Karenni 10.3%<br>Burman 2.8%<br>Mon 0.7%<br>Other 7% |

**Source: TBC (December, 2014)**

TBC maintains a database which includes all registered and unregistered refugees and is shared with the UNHCR to ensure compatibility. The database is updated monthly for births, deaths, departures, and new arrivals, to create the "verified caseload." Food rations are distributed only to those who show up in person to receive their supplies. The actual number of people fed each month is known as the "feeding figure." According to the December 2014 figures, the verified caseload in the camps was 110,607 and the feeding figure 108,583. As nearly 100,000 have been resettled to third countries, current numbers do not represent the overall population that has fled to the camps over the years.

In the camps, refugees have limited educational and training opportunities and no official means of earning an income. While education in the camps is far better than any education available to civilians inside Burma, there are limited opportunities for higher education, which also largely remains unrecognised outside the camps. Karen and other ethnic peoples of Burma traditionally place a very high value on education and many have crossed the border to Thailand in order to go to a camp school. Although the majority of the camp populations have arrived as a family unit (TBC, 2012a), many parents also send their children to attend schools in refugee camps across the Thai border (KHRG, 2008).

*"If we had stayed in the village, we knew that our children could never attend school and I wanted my children to go to school to be educated people. We also didn't have any house to stay in. We could only stay in the forest and we had to flee away when the SPDC came or patrolled around our area, so we decided it was better to go to the refugee camp." (Saw P—, a 47-year-old male from P— village, Papun District; KHRG, 2008, p. 58)*

With more than 40,000 residents, Mae La is the biggest of the refugee camps on the Thailand-Burma border. Due to its size and easily accessibly location, Mae La is considered a centre of study for refugees. Mae La's current population includes 1,039 boarding house students who have come to study in the camp mostly from Burma. In total, as of July 2014 there were 2,763 boarding house students in the camps (TBC, 2014a). Many other students also stay with their relatives in the camps.

The issue for many young students is what happens after they finish a post-ten school, the highest level of education available in most of the camps. There are only a handful of schools on the Thailand-Burma border where these young students can apply for, leaving thousands of talented and dedicated aspiring university students with no means to educate themselves.

**Countless of people have learned about their own history as well as to read and write their own language in the camps. (Photo: Liz Bordo)**

Education in the camps is provided by CBOs such as the Karen Refugee Committee – Education Entity (KRC-EE) backed up by international NGOs such as World Education. Many schools, especially in the less remote camps in Tak Province, have foreign teachers and volunteers, majority of whom stay illegally in the camps as permits remain largely unattainable. These foreigners teach refugees English and other subjects while hiding from Thai authorities, risking fines or even deportation. After the Thai junta took over power in May 2014, however, it has become increasingly difficult to enter and stay in the camps without a permit.

Educational opportunities also vary greatly from one camp to the next. In the more remote camps such as Mae La Oon in Mae Hong Son Province and Ban Don Yang in Kanchanaburi Province, situation is dire as higher education remains largely unattainable, and education institutions far away out of reach. Most of the opportunities are available either in the Tak camps – Mae La, Umpiem Mai and Nu Po – or in the border town of Mae Sot.

One of the most prestigious of the schools available for refugees is the Australian Catholic University (ACU), which offers a Diploma in Liberal Studies in Mae Sot as well as in Ranong. Other commendable schools include the Wide Horizons and Minmahaw GED Programmes in Mae Sot, English Immersion Program in Umpiem Mai, and Global Border Studies Programme in Nu Po. As these opportunities are only available to a few students each year, thousands of capable young adults are left with no means to pursue their dream of higher education. Many young people are determined to help their people and their country, but with no place to go for study, they often end up opening a shop or becoming a nurse or a teacher in the camp. Some leave to find factory work in Bangkok or elsewhere in Thailand while many others turn to drugs and alcohol as they see their dreams crushed before them.

Having lived in a place where freedom of movement as well as self-expression is severely restricted, many young refugees feel scared about leaving the refugee camps even to pursue higher education in other camps on the border. Most have heard stories about the police check points and intimidation by Thai authorities that sometimes takes place even when refugees have managed to obtain travel documents (Human Rights Watch, 2012b). Others have already experienced being thrown to a detention centre and are reluctant to take the risk of leaving the camps.

International organisations such as the UNHCR, the United Nations Children's Fund (UNICEF) and the International Committee of the Red Cross (ICRC) have also faced restrictions in Thailand that have made it difficult for them to provide even rudimentary protection for those who have crossed the border to Thailand (see Human Rights Watch, 2007). The framework of international principles that recognises the inherent dignity and the equal and inalienable rights of all members of the human family to be universally protected have little significance to refugees who live in Thailand.

The 1951 United Nations Convention lays down basic minimum standards for the treatment of refugees, including access to the courts, to primary education, and to work (UNHCR, 2010). The Convention defines a refugee as a person who:

*"...owing to well-founded fear of being persecuted for reasons of race, religion, nationality, membership of a particular social group or political opinion, is outside the country of his nationality and is unable or, owing to such fear, is unwilling to avail himself of the protection of that country; or who, not having a nationality and being outside the country of his former habitual residence as a result of such events, is unable or, owing to such fear, is unwilling to return to it."*

Thailand is not a party to the 1951 Convention or its 1967 Protocol. For 30 years now, Thailand's policy has been to confine the "persons of concern" to their "temporary shelters" until the situation in Burma would improve and the displaced could go home. The Burmese government has also consistently denied having any problems associated with refugees. In 2003, the government published a highly controversial statement:

*"As Myanmar is not engaged in any war with other countries, there is no problem of refugees. The armed insurrection groups also have come back into the legal fold and there is peace in the country." (Government of Burma, 2003, p. 54, IX A art.22 / 217)*

While the UNHCR publically maintains that "...the generosity of the Royal Thai Government in hosting refugees and asylum-seekers has spanned several decades (UNHCR, 2012)," others have described Thailand's refugee policies as "fragmented, unpredictable, inadequate and ad hoc (e.g. Human Rights Watch, 2012b, p. 1)." Even UNHCR goes on to explain how they operate in a challenging environment, which is characterised by inadequate protection space for many persons of concern. Although UNHCR normally promotes three durable solutions for refugees; repatriation to their home countries, local integration in the host country, or resettlement to third countries, none of these solutions were available in Thailand until 2004 (TBC, 2012a), twenty years after the first refugees had arrived from Burma.

Thai authorities allowed refugees to register with the UNHCR periodically during 2004 and 2005, and since 2005, all registered refugees have been eligible for resettlement to third countries. In June 2014, 96,206 had been resettled, vast majority (75%) of them to the US, followed by Australia, Canada, Finland, and Norway (TBC, 2014a). Departures for resettlement have declined each year since 2008, mainly because the majority of those who were able to register have already left. The group settlement programme to the US has now closed, but a significant number remain in the pipeline and are expected to depart in 2015 (TBC, 2014a).

**Camp residents live in bamboo houses as they are not allowed to use permanent building materials. (Photo: Liz Bordo)**

Of the current camp residents, 38% are not registered and thus ineligible for resettlement (TBC, September, 2014). Refugees also have numerous concerns regarding resettlement that often lead to eligible refugees staying in the camps. One of the common issues is the inability to organise family reunions when resettled refugees have children that are over the age of 18. Those who have been resettled often have done so in order to provide for their families and relatives in the camps. Refugees typically maintain close links with the camps and frequently send money to their loved ones. According to the Human Rights Watch (2012b), despite the UNHCR having a presence on the border since 1998, its role in the camps is extremely limited. Human Rights Watch adds that "The agency has demonstrated little ability to counter the Thai government's ad hoc policies of containment and provides virtually no protection to Burmese asylum seekers outside the camps (p. 19)."

**Refugees plead for UN registration on the World Refugee Day in June 2012, Mae La refugee camp. (Photo: Burma Link)**

As a result of inadequate protection of refugees, as well as the highly restricted life in the camps, thousands live in the country as illegal aliens. Many Burman nationals who have fled their home country, including most former (forcibly conscripted) child soldiers in the Burma Army, also remain outside the refugee camps because they fear they may be ostracised by the refugee population who has fled Burma Army (most of whom are Burman) abuses and who are usually of a different ethnicity. Many Burman refugees in the camps talk about problems of discrimination, exclusion, and suspicions of being government spies, often leading them to depart the camps. Other camp residents, who speak Burmese language, have also faced similar problems as they have been mistaken for being Burman. Refugees belonging to minority groups, however, say that the situation has improved in recent years and refugees are mostly not afraid to speak Burmese anymore.

Due to the refugees in the camps being forced to be nearly completely dependent on outside help for food, shelter, protection and other basic needs, their coping mechanisms have been severely eroded. Travel and work restrictions have had adverse psychological and social effects on the refugees, decreasing their self-sufficiency, camp morale and mental health (TBC, 2012a).

*"Living in the camp is similar to living in prison because I can't go outside or make my own decision. I can commute only in the camp. The camp is surrounded by barbed wire. If we go outside of the camp, Thai police will arrest us. In the long run, it affects not only my physical but also my mental health." (Christine, 22, Karen refugee, spoke with Burma Link in Mae La refugee camp in May 2014; Burma Link, 2014b)*

In a 2006 study, PU-AMI found that 50% of adult camp residents suffer from mental health problems and anti-depressants constituted one of the most common drug prescriptions for refugees (as cited in Human Rights Watch, 2012b, p. 19). Halting long-term sustainability prospects in the camps has also created a climate where refugees tend to think only short-term, from one ration to another. Some refugees have adapted this form of thinking already back in Burma where many were forced to flee Burma Army attacks from one hiding site to another. When the refugees will eventually return to Burma, many of them will need assistance not only in skills to sustain themselves but also in changing their thinking from short-term survival to long-term development. In a similar vein, those who have remained in hiding inside the country have been on the run for so long that many consider it normal to regularly flee and hide from government forces and to build a new village after another.

Considering the often traumatic backgrounds as well as the challenging circumstances that refugees face in Thailand, many people who visit the camps are impressed by the significant effort refugees make in order to maintain dignity and hope in the camp communities. Despite severe restrictions and depressive realities, refugees strive to remain active and to maintain their cultural traditions through practices such as teaching ethnic nationality languages, histories, and dances. People marry and have children, play sports, and organise festivals and other celebrations. Despite the devastating reality, life goes on. Thousands of people of Burma have come to consider these enclosed areas as their homes, trying to lead their lives as the best they can.

*"From the beginning I was moved by the faith and dignity of the refugees I met, their determination to get on with their lives as best as they could, and their apparent belief that somehow, someday, justice would be done." (Jack Dunford, Executive Director of TBC 1984-2012; TBC, 2013a)*

**Monks playing caneball in Mae La refugee camp. (Photo: Liz Bordo)**

While vast majority of refugees in the camps are ethnic Karen from eastern Burma, camps also vary greatly with regard to ethnic diversity. Umpiem Mai and Nu Po are the most ethnically diverse with over 20% of the camp populations comprising of non-Karen or Karenni ethnic groups. Mae Ra Ma Luang, Mae La Oon, and Tham Hin are the most homogenous with ethnic Karen comprising 99% of the populations (TBC, 2013b). Literacy rate in the camps is estimated as 60% (TBC, 2013b).

When living in the camps, one will notice the integral part that religion plays in most refugees' lives. Religious buildings are centres of communal activities and refugees regularly attend religious ceremonies, sing and listen to religious songs, and read religious texts. Prayers are often said before meals, and in many Christian schools before the beginning of each school day.

Most refugees in the camps are either Christian (51%) or Buddhist (36%). In the Tak camps, however, there are also significant Muslim communities. Muslims have been successful in setting up businesses in the camps, particularly noticeable in Mae La camp, where the main market has only one shop maintained by an ethnic Karen, the rest being run by Muslims.

Most of the camps are isolated in the mountains and at the end of dirt roads, while some camps, such as Mae La and Umpiem Mai, are located as close as 1 to 1.5 hour drive away from the nearest town of Mae Sot. The isolated camps tend to be far away from hospitals and some have no phone signal. The realities in the remote camps are very different from the easily accessible camps that also have much more opportunities for study and work. In these camps almost all residents are de facto refugees, as the camps have had very little pull factor other than safety from the Burmese military.

Three of the camps (Mae La, Tham Hin, and Ban Don Yang) are overcrowded (Human Rights Watch, 2012b). In all camps, the challenge of space is a significant concern. When living in one of the camps one will notice the almost complete lack of personal space or privacy. In some areas of the camps, houses are built right next to each other, people are everywhere, and it seems to never be quiet as there is always someone in the earshot singing, playing music, listening to the radio, or simply talking. Refugees who still have memories of life in Burma struggle to adapt to having no space around their houses; "Here, it is like fifty villages are crammed into one," one refugee told TBC (2004, p. 53).

Due to space restrictions and limited housing supplies provided in the camps, many households comprise more than one family and young married couples typically continue to live with their parents. Space restrictions coupled with bamboo building materials also make camps into "fire traps" and despite refugees being aware of the danger, fires regularly sweep through the communities. In February 2012, a huge fire in Umpiem camp destroyed as many as 1,000 houses (Karen News, February, 2012). In April 2013, 36 refugees died in a tragic fire that destroyed Ban Mae Surin refugee camp in Mae Hong Son Province. In December 2013, around 750 refugees were left homeless in Mae La camp when more than a hundred houses were destroyed by a fire. The next day one refugee woman died in a fire in Ban Mai Nai Soi camp.

**Mae La Zone C after the fire on December 27, 2013. (Photo: Eugene/Burma Link AOC)**

Although some basic health care is provided in the camps, diseases such as malaria, dengue fever and tuberculosis are still common among the refugees. According to TBC (2014a), the border-wide average chronic (stunting) malnutrition rate is classified as "very high," with camps with the highest stunting rates being located in the most remote areas of the border.

The camps are highly organised with regularly elected camp leaders, committees, and section leaders, although refugees regularly complain about corruption and lack of transparency in the leadership. The Karen Refugee Committee (KRC) and the Karenni Refugee Committee (KnRC) are the overall representatives of the refugees living in the camps. These Committees coordinate and oversee all camp activities through the Camp Committees, coordinate assistance provided by NGOs, and liaise with UNHCR, Thai authorities, and security personnel (TBC, 2013a). Each camp is headed by one leader whilst hundreds of people serve on the Camp Committees, organising the storage and distribution of rations, safeguarding the camps' physical environment and infrastructure, and overseeing health clinics, the school system, and the administration of justice (TBC, 2004).

The latest Refugee Committee and Camp Committee elections were held in early 2013. According to TBC (2013a), all registered and unregistered refugees over the age of 20, regardless of gender, religion and ethnicity, were able to vote. Camp residents, however, voiced concerns over the elections. According to one young refugee who spoke with Burma Link, "Most people don't know whether they are eligible to vote or not. So, most unregistered didn't vote."

A variety of CBOs formed by members of the refugee communities also support specific social groups, such as the Karenni Students Union, the Karen Youth Organisation, and the Karen Handicapped Welfare Association. Refugee women's organisations have been particularly active in advocating for women's rights and the participation of women in all aspects of society.

TBC remains the only agency responsible for providing food and shelter assistance to the refugees in the camps. In the past, TBC also regularly purchased and distributed blankets, mosquito nets, clothing for children under five and thread for longyi weaving, sleeping mats, and cooking pots both to current and newly arrived camp residents. Recent funding cuts on the border have forced TBC to cease the provision of all non-food items even to new arrivals. Only cooking stoves and donated items are still being distributed to refugees. As a consequence of the funding cuts, TBC's food rations have also fallen substantially below minimum daily nutritional levels (see TBC, 2013a). Health and education services for the refugees have also been cut back, having an adverse effect on the camp residents.

As the recent restrictions in movement have strictly prohibited refugees from leaving camp premises, the reduced rations have become a grave concern. According to the refugees themselves (based on Burma Link's interviews in December 2014 and January 2015), it is the poorest and the most vulnerable who suffer the consequences as they are not able to go to the forest to hunt for rats and collect vegetables, nor to buy extra food as they are now not allowed to take on work as daily workers. Some refugees are now employing more risky behaviours and strategies in order to bridge the widened gap between their basic needs and the humanitarian assistance they receive. While some households are able to supplement their needs through economic activities, others are simply no longer able to meet their needs.

In order to cope with the situation, TBC has employed a method of identifying food secure and insecure households in order to implement Community Managed Targeting, in which self-reliant refugees will forfeit their rations whilst the most vulnerable receive extra supplies (see TBC, 2013a). Eye-witness accounts, however, tell a grim story. Burma Link has received reports of some refugees believing they are being starved out in order to avoid their continuing assistance and future repatriation.

Many refugees refuse to settle for their faith as helpless and passive victims and are making great efforts to cope and provide for their families through taking part in different livelihood activities, when possible. Some international NGOs and local CBOs such as TBC provide the refugees with opportunities for skills training and income generation, although these projects reach only a small part of refugee populations. Refugees are also often left frustrated as after taking part in the trainings, they have nowhere to use their newly-found skills. Some have taken part in one TBC training after another, unable to apply their skills in practice.

TBC does, however, have several successful projects in the camps such as the Community Agriculture Programme (CAP) that is currently implemented in eight camps (TBC, 2014a). CAP gardening activities are important in that they increase the availability of fresh food in camps, and prepare refugees with vital livelihood skills. As a result of CAP activities, hundreds of households in the camps are now able to cultivate their own gardens. TBC also supports some projects run by local CBOs on Burma side of the border, e.g. the Back Pack Health Worker Team's (BPHWT) water supply and sanitation projects and the Karen Human Rights Group's (KHRG's) village agency project.

Other organisations also undertake training activities in the camps. COERR, for example, has trained refugees on appropriate and sustainable organic agricultural practices, assisted refugee communities to develop basic social work technical skills, and provided vocational training for individuals in extremely vulnerable situations (see *COERR – Project*).

These activities, when successfully implemented, are essential for the refugees to regain confidence, motivation, and a sense of independence from external aid. They will also be extremely valuable for refugees if they return to Burma or are resettled in third countries. Since 2005, the UNHCR and CCSDPT have advocated with the Thai authorities for a relaxation in the policy of confinement to camps (see TBC, 2013a). The policy nevertheless remains in place and restrictions have recently been tightened. While many refugees make significant efforts to remain active in the challenging and often depressive situation, the vast majority of camp residents are increasingly reliant on outside support and aid as a result of forced passivity.

The recent political changes and ceasefire talks in Burma have resulted in widespread and grossly premature talks of repatriating the refugees. Only one month after Burma transitioned to a nominally civilian government in March 2011, Thai authorities announced that they are in the process of discussion with the Burmese government about closing the refugee camps (Chitradon, April, 2011). More recently, the Thai junta announced that it wants to repatriate all refugees by 2015 (Saw Yan Naing, July, 2014b). These are grave concerns for the refugees as major obstacles for safe repatriation remain. In fact, none of the reasons why refugees fled have seen a sustainable solution; peace process has stalled, ceasefires remain fragile and unpredictable, landmine contamination is among the worst in the world, health and education is lacking, poverty is rampant, and human rights violations continue (see e.g. Davis, Gittleman, Sollom, Richards, & Beyrer, 2012; KHRG, 2014; ND-Burma, 2013, 2014a, 2014b).

Although the consensus is that conditions are not yet conducive for refugees to return, TBC has recently changed their focus to preparedness for refugee and IDP return (TBC, 2013a, 2014a). Talks about repatriation coupled with reduced aid and increased restrictions have caused anxiety and uncertainty among the refugees who do not feel safe returning to their homeland.

While it is hoped that the international donor community will be willing to continue necessary support on the border until the time is right for refugees to return, a major current challenge is that many NGOs and CBOs along the border are struggling to sustain even basic services to refugees as donors are shifting their funds inside Burma. One can only hope that agencies such as the UNHCR will respect its public commitments and "ensure that repatriation is voluntary, undertaken in safety and dignity, and takes place only when conditions are conducive (UNHCR, 2013)."

**Children in Umpiem Mai (Photo: Burma Link)**

## Further Reading

• For more information on how TBC became involved on the Thailand-Burma border and for a comprehensive history of the border as well as an overview of life in the refugee camps;

TBC (2004). *Between worlds: Twenty years on the border.* The Border Consortium.

## In Exile outside the Camps

It is estimated that at least 80% of as many as three million migrant workers in Thailand are from Burma (TBC, 2012a). Many organisations such as the Human Rights Watch, IRC and TBC are concerned that a large number of the Burmese[3] migrants in Thailand are de facto refugees, having fled due to the same circumstances as those living in the camps (see e.g. Green-Rauenhorst et al., 2008; Human Rights Watch, 2012b; TBC, 2012a). While it is impossible to know how many of the Burmese living in Thailand outside of camps are de facto refugees, research suggests that only a small number of those who warrant refugee status actually receive any aid or protection.

**Two sisters who have experienced the conflict first-hand and now live in a Karen village on the Thai side of the border. (Photo: Burma Link)**

In 2006, IRC conducted an interview survey of 1,704 Burmese living in border areas of Thailand, aiming to document the migrants' experiences and assessing the degree to which they merit international

[3] The term Burmese is used to refer to all people of Burma regardless of ethnicity.

protection as refugees (Green-Rauenhorst et al., 2008). Results revealed many stories of these migrants sharing similar threads of violence, displacement due to conflict, and fear of return. In a similar vein, Human Rights Watch reported in 2012 that many of the Burmese interviewees living outside the camps were refugees who had chosen to risk detention and deportation in order avoid the humiliation and dependency of camp life (Human Rights Watch, 2012b). Indeed, when talking with people of Burma in villages on the border, it becomes clear that many refugees have chosen to live in villages, even with great struggles to make a living and far away from hospitals, to keep some degree of freedom and a sense of independency.

Refugees in Thailand face a stark choice. They can either live confined to one of the camps on the border and be relatively protected from arrest and deportation, or live outside the camps with the freedom to work but typically with no legal documents. As a result of the inadequate protection and registration of refugees, as well as the highly restricted life in the refugee camps, scores of refugees choose to live in the country as illegal aliens.

Some refugees, many of them ethnic Shan and Mon, have not even had a choice to live in a camp. Unlike on the borders of Karen and Karenni States, there are no official refugee camps along the Thailand-Shan border. According to a report by SHRF and SWAN (2002), Thai policy recognises only "temporarily displaced persons" fleeing directly from fighting, and not from the abuses inflicted on civilian populations by the Burmese military's anti-insurgency campaigns. Therefore, the estimated population of over 150,000 Shan refugees, who fled to Thailand following the forced relocation in central Shan State in 1996, have been denied any protection and humanitarian assistance and have been forced to find work as migrant labourers. The report by SHRF and SWAN clearly demonstrates how lots of Shan exiles have a genuine fear of persecution.

Ethnic Mon people also represent very small numbers of the refugee camp residents despite the fact that thousands of Mon have fled conflicts and abuse in their land. With no majority-Mon refugee camps on Thailand's soil, many Mon either live as IDPs on the Burma side of the border, or as undocumented migrants outside the camps. Similarly to other undocumented refugees in Thailand, all of these people are liable for arrest, detention, and deportation at any time.

In 2002, the IRC reported that over 19,000 undocumented Burmese migrants were arrested and deported over a four month period (Green-Rauenhorst et al., 2008). Many of them were sent directly to the SPDC [State Peace and Development Council, as the regime was known at the time] reception centre in Myawaddi, opposite to Mae Sot in Tak Province. Interrogations are known to be conducted in the centre, which in turn have been directly linked to torture and other severe ill treatment in Burma (see e.g. AAPP, 2011; ND-Burma, 2012a).

Since 2004, Thailand has offered migrant workers, who play an important role in the Thai economy, the opportunity to register and receive temporary work permits. Having a work permit can still be entirely dependent on the migrants' willingness and ability to pay and sometimes Thai employers may not be willing to go through the process with their employees. In 2009, the Thai government began to institute a new system of registering migrant workers, requiring undocumented migrants to first undergo a Nationality Verification process with their own governments (see Human Rights Watch, 2012b). For many people of Burma, however, returning back to their home country is not an option.

Many undocumented migrants carry a variety of documents, many of which have no legal validity. Some migrant worker ID cards are also locally issued informal work permits that bar the bearer from traveling outside the province where the migrant worker is registered. Burmese migrants have voiced added concerns over the cost of the documents, fraudulent documents, and corruption (see e.g. Human Rights Watch, 2012b). Even where there are rules, the rules are often bent, and even with all the correct documents, migrants might still get in trouble. In July 2014, TBC reported that well over 1.5 million Burmese migrant workers in Thailand remained undocumented (TBC, 2014a).

*"I can't solve these problems and be free from these troubles. The only way is to flee into Thailand and search for a job as a migrant worker."(Shan man, Mong Nai Township, interviewed in June 2008; TBC, 2008, p. 26)*

In recent years, the Thai authorities have stepped up their efforts and taken more measures to address undocumented migrant workers and human trafficking by establishing service centres across the country where undocumented migrants can register and receive temporary work permits (TBC, 2014a).

Thailand has also allowed an impressive amount of work to be undertaken on the border with the aim of building a better Burma for future generations. The border is home to numerous local organisations set up by refugees and migrants from Burma. Although these organisations are typically divided along ethnic lines, there is also a high degree of cooperation and networking between the groups as well as inter-ethnic diversity within the organisations.

The scope of local women organisations on the border is particularly impressive considering the circumstances these women have experienced in their home country. Some of these organisations include the Kachin Women's Association Thailand, Karen Women's Organisation, Palaung Women's Organisation, and Shan Women's Action Network. Since 1999, eleven ethnic women's organisations have joined together under the umbrella of Women's League of Burma (WLB), which aims to increase the participation of women in the struggle for democracy and human rights, promoting women's participation in the national peace and reconciliation process, and enhancing the role of the women of Burma at the national and international levels (see WLB, 2011).

The Thailand-Burma border, during the past decades, has become home not only to scores of Burmese exiles who have fled their home for numerous reasons, but also to a highly organised movement that works towards a free, peaceful, and democratic Burma.

## Further Reading

• For more information on Thailand's treatment of refugees and asylum seekers;

Human Rights Watch (2012b). *Ad Hoc and Inadequate. Thailand's Treatment of Refugees and Asylum Seekers*. Human Rights Watch report, September 2012. © 2012 by Human Rights Watch.

## Displaced in Burma

Internally displaced persons (IDPs) are often wrongly called refugees. Unlike refugees, IDPs have not crossed an international border but remain displaced inside their home country. Even though they have generally fled for similar reasons as refugees (armed conflict, persecution, and human rights abuse), IDPs legally remain under the protection of their own government. In Burma, they are thus in an extremely vulnerable position as they are supposed to be protected by the same government that's military troops are usually the cause of their flight. The existence of international laws and regulations means nothing to the hundreds of thousands of people in Burma who try to survive in the jungle with little help from the international community.

**A child looking after his young brother in a hiding site in Lu Thaw Township, Papun District. (Photo: KHRG)**

*"Even though we are not safe here, I don't want to leave and stay in a refugee camp. I just want to live in my village." (Karenni male, KSWDC focus group, Pasaung Township, June 2008; TBC, 2008, p. 11)*

Accurate figures for IDPs are difficult to determine due to poor access to affected areas. The UNHCR estimates that there are 587,000 IDPs in Burma (UNHCR, 2015b), however the IDMC estimates that there were 643,000 IDPs due to conflict and violence in Burma as of July 2014 (IDMC, 2014). According to both IDMC (2014) and TBC (2013c), an estimated 400,000 of the internally displaced reside in southeast Burma. Only a fraction of them, 12,639 in December 2014, live in IDP camps (TBC, December, 2014). Vast majority have to manage without any protection or aid apart from help from some small local ethnic organisations that mostly operate from across the border from Thailand.

The historical ceasefire agreement signed between the KNU and the government in January 2012 filled many IDPs with hope that the generations-old conflict might finally come to an end. Largely due to this, approximately 37,000 formerly displaced persons attempted to either return to their villages or resettle in surrounding areas of southeast Burma between August 2011 and July 2012 (TBC, 2012b). During the same period, however, over 10,000 people were still forced from their homes, according to the same TBC report. More recently, the movement has slowed down; during the twelve months prior to July 2014, over 9,900 IDPs were identified as having return into their former villages or resettled elsewhere, whilst 4,200 were newly displaced (TBC, 2014b).

Most IDPs in eastern Burma have been forced to flee their homes due to the same reasons as refugees; armed conflicts between ethnic armed groups and government forces and the grave human rights violations and war crimes committed primarily by the Burma Army. Particularly in the ethnic outlying areas adjacent to Thailand, Burma Army has undertaken massive counter-insurgency campaigns in line with their Four Cuts policy, deliberately targeting ethnic civilians and resulting in systematic and widespread abuse and the destruction of thousands of communities. Since 1996, more than 3,700 villages have been documented as destroyed, forcibly relocated, or abandoned (TBC, 2012b). Many have argued that the actions of the Burma Army in the ethnic states count as genocide (see e.g. La Guardia, June, 2005; Rogers, 2004). Meanwhile, the Burmese military has continuously denied that its soldiers have abused civilians (e.g. RFA, March 2013).

While ceasefires between some notable ethnic armies and the government have resulted in less direct attacks on civilians in eastern Burma in recent years (TBC, 2013a), reports indicate that violations of international humanitarian law have persisted throughout the country since the Thein Sein administration took office in March 2011 (e.g. Davis et al., 2012; ND-Burma, 2012b, 2013, 2014a, 2014b). The KHRG report published in March 2013 indicates that natural resource extraction and business projects have fuelled human rights violations even after the ceasefire was signed between the government and the KNU (KHRG, 2013). According to the TBC report from November 2014, "Land confiscation is linked to the consolidation of garrisons, road construction and the establishment of new concessions for mining, logging and commercial agriculture (TBC, 2014b)."

**Mon family making floor brooms in a Mon IDP camp Halockhani, located only one kilometer from the refugee camp Ban Don Yang in Kanchanaburi Province, Thailand. (Photo: Ariana Zarleen)**

Skirmishes have not stopped either, primarily due to the lack of Burma Army troop withdrawals from sensitive areas. Although villagers in the Karen State can now travel more freely, land grabbing and drug trade has increased, and Burma Army has been fortifying their positions in Karen areas (KHRG, 2014), bringing to question their commitment to peace. It seems that while the government is talking peace, their troops are preparing for war. Continuing Burma Army attacks and large scale offensives in northern Burma also shed doubt on the peace process. In Kachin and Shan States, Burma Army continues to abuse ethnic civilians much in the same way as they did in eastern Burma before. As long as the conflict and abuse continues anywhere in the country, and the political goals of the ethnic nationalities are not discussed, it is only a matter of time until conflict reignites in eastern Burma. The latest conflicts in the Karen State forcing thousands to flee their homes took place as recently as in September and October 2014, showing the fragility of the ceasefires.

Many ethnic civilians and the ethnic armed groups were hopeful and positive about the peace process and reforms in Burma until recently. Tensions have risen as it has begun to dawn on people that the government may not be genuine in their efforts to build peace and a federal union. The living conditions in the ethnic borderlands in eastern Burma also remain as dire as ever, despite marked improvements in majority Burman central areas of Burma, particularly cities like Rangoon and Mandalay. TBC's comprehensive IDP survey in 2012 found that more than half of the people in the rural communities of southeast Burma were impoverished, most of them lacked access to safe drinking water, and a third of children between five and twelve years of age were not regularly attending school (TBC, 2012b). A less comprehensive survey conducted in 2013 suggested similar results (TBC, 2013c).

The United Nations "Guiding Principles on Internal Displacement" provides authoritative standards for the obligations of governments to IDPs. Under the principles, the authorities are to provide displaced people at a minimum with safe access to essential food and potable water, basic shelter and housing, appropriate clothing, and essential medical services and sanitation (Principal 18: UN OCHA, 2004, pp. 9-10). IDPs in Burma, however, have little access to any of these (US State Department, 2013). Displacement in Burma has also been linked to poverty and poor health outcomes, including increased malaria prevalence, child malnutrition and child mortality (The Human Rights Center & The Center for Public Health and Human Rights, 2007).

While the UNHCR assisted some 312,000 IDPs inside Burma in January (UNHCR, 2015b), hundreds of thousands of others live in the mountains and the jungle under desperate circumstances, often moving from one hiding site to another, collecting leaves, roots and anything they can find in order to survive. Although decades of fleeing and displacement have resulted in many communities developing creative strategies to cope with the situation, humanitarian needs of IDPs include food and other necessities, such as medicine, blankets, warm clothing, firewood and fuel, and adequate shelter. A range of civil society actors, especially local CBOs and ethnic organisations such as the Karen Office of Relief and Development (KORD) and the KNU, have worked to deliver aid to IDPs.

**New housing for IDPs in the Karen State built by KNU. (Photo: Burma Link)**

Most of these organisations are based in Thailand, from where they have arranged cross-border aid to some of the poorest and most oppressed areas in Burma. Cross-border delivery of aid has been essential for IDP survival for over 20 years, and due to the proximity of many IDPs to Thailand, combined with the difficulty of reaching them from inside Burma, it will continue to be relevant in the future. While there has been a recent relaxation of government restrictions on access into some conflict-affected areas in southeast Burma (TBC, 2012b), most communities remain out of reach from inside. Recent funding cuts on the border have, regrettably, forced many organisations such as the KORD to cut back on crucial assistance to IDPs (Saw Yan Naing, May, 2012).

Since the reforms started in 2011, there has been renewed optimism that the recent developments could bring about an end to the armed conflicts between the government and a number of ethnic armed groups.

*"We have great hopes for peace but we still have doubts about the process. We can't trust the ceasefire agreement 100%, but only about 50%. If the ceasefire can be sustained, people's livelihoods will become more stable. There hasn't been much change in the short period so far, but at least we can say that we are more confident." (Karenni Woman, Phruso Township, June 2012, KSWDC interview; TBC, 2012b, p. 18)*

Recent stalling or even backtracking of the reform process and lack of genuine political dialogue is, however, increasingly burying the dreams for genuine peace in the near future. For sustainable peace to become reality, ceasefires will need to move to genuine political dialogue, and the deep-seated mistrust that the displaced people of Burma have developed towards the government and its military will need to be addressed. The government of Burma must acknowledge that torture and other violations are taking place, take steps to end these practices, address the complex needs of survivors, and end impunity. Acknowledging victims and survivors of past abuses will be a key for national reconciliation.

*"If this peace agreement breaks down, our life will be worse than before. In our history, we have been cheated by the Burmans many times. We do not trust them, and the Burmans do not trust us. Our ancestors said that when we eat fruit from a fig tree, we should also listen for arrows. We have to be cautious." (Karen man, Dawei Township, June 2012, CIDKP focus group discussion; TBC, 2012b, p. 12)*

*"I don't dare to go back to my original village or to rebuild in a new village yet. In 2004 when KNU and the Government established a gentlemen's agreement, I started cultivating a hillside paddy field close to the road. But the agreement broke down and I had to run deeper into the forest again. So I don't know if I can trust the Tatmadaw this time." (Karen Man, Hpapun Township, May 2012, KORD focus group discussion; TBC, 2012b, p. 40)*

As Burma has undergone a number of changes during the past years, there are now hopes that conditions might be developed into such that IDPs and refugees may at last be able to go home. Meanwhile, it is imperative that the humanitarian needs of hundreds of thousands of IDPs are not forgotten, and movement back to the displaced persons' former villages is not encouraged until there is genuine and lasting peace.

## Further Reading

• For more information on poverty and displacement in southeast Burma;

TBC (2012b). *Changing Realities, Poverty and Displacement in South East Burma/Myanmar – 2012 Survey*. The Border Consortium.

## Recent Funding Cuts on the Border

Due to all the positive media attention that Thein Sein and his government have received, there is a spreading belief among international donors that Burma is soon to be a free and peaceful country. Whilst ceasefire agreements have indeed been signed with several ethnic armed groups, these ceasefires remain fragile and unpredictable, the peace process has stalled, fighting rages on in Kachin and Shan States, human rights violations continue, around 400,000 remain internally displaced in southeast Burma, and 110,000 still reside in refugee camps on the Thailand-Burma border.

International donors have, however, recently been pouring resources into central Burma without considering the needs that local CBOs on the Thailand-Burma border have been addressing for decades. Regrettably, much of this funding increase has come at a cost for ethnic organisations along the border (Naw Noreen, July, 2013; Saw Yan Naing, May, 2012). According to Kevin Malseed, programme manager for the Canadian social justice organisation, Inter Pares, "Cutting off assistance to border-based and cross-border groups to channel aid only through Rangoon would throw away the positive results of 20 years of support (Saw Yan Naing, May, 2012)." He added that "it is extremely naïve and counterproductive to drop cross-border aid and initiatives to 'reinvent the wheel in Rangoon.' " With several aid organisations and nations cutting support to organisations based along the Thailand-Burma border, nearly everyone on the border has been affected. The work of ethnic and government-critical organisations has been severely hampered, and the people on the border have been increasingly silenced.

Widespread cuts have not spared long-standing aid providers such as the Mae Tao Clinic (MTC) in Mae Sot, which issued an emergency funding appeal in July 2012 after treating hundreds of thousands of Burmese patients for free for over two decades. The situation worsened significantly in November 2013 when the Australian government announced that it will cut all of the AUSD 450,000 funding it gives to the clinic due to shifting their priority to prepare for refugee repatriation (Karen News, November, 2013). Whilst it is frightening that the Australian government would spend a significant amount to prepare for premature repatriation, shifting aid is also a huge setback for the thousands of people who keep travelling great distances to receive medical treatment at the clinic. Dr. Cynthia Maung – the legendary founder of the MTC who ironically was in Australia receiving an award when she received the devastating news – pointed out that it will be years before Burma's under funded health infrastructure will be capable of properly treating its citizens.

TBC has also been severely affected by funding cuts, which have forced the consortium to cut food rations and cease the provision of all non-food items, with the exception of cooking stoves and donated items, even to new arrivals (TBC, 2013a). In September 2013, TBC announced cutting food rations to refugees due to reductions in funding (TBC, September, 2013). Refugees say it is becoming increasingly difficult to survive in the camps and many now face a bleak situation feeling forced to return to Burma. Many local organisations, such as the KWO, have also condemned the funding cuts affecting refugees (Karen News, May, 2014). Furthermore, as the Thailand-Burma border is where many organisations work to arrange aid to the poorest and most oppressed areas in southeast Burma, funding cuts on the border have affected the aid reaching vulnerable IDPs.

In early April 2012, 26 Burmese frontier organisations gathered in Chiang Mai for a meeting to discuss the future of cross-border aid and appeal for fresh donations from charity groups (Lawi Weng, April, 2012). In June 2013, more than 150 representatives and observers from 40 Karen organisations from inside Burma, along the Thailand-Burma border, and overseas, voiced their concern that there has been a significant decrease in humanitarian aid for communities at risk in the Karen State (Karen News, June, 2013). The KWO and the Karen Education Department (KED), for example, said that international humanitarian aid that they have been receiving has decreased by as much as a half. The representatives strongly urged the international community to continue its cross-border humanitarian assistance until real peace is achieved in Burma.

Burmese migrant children studying in Thailand are also seeing their dreams evaporate as international aid dries up and organisations abandon the people on the border in favour of initiatives inside the country (Bangkok Post, May, 2012). More than two dozen migrant schools in western Thailand have faced closure as international donors continued to slash funding for groups on the border, a local NGO warned in July, 2013 (Naw Noreen, July, 2013). In 2014, even more donor organisations stopped providing financial support to migrant schools (S' Phan Shaung, August, 2014).

Thailand-Burma border is also where most of the capacity building and pro-democracy work has been done. It is ironic that as Burma takes steps towards becoming more democratic, it is the pro-democracy movement that should suffer.

**Thailand-Burma border is home to hundreds of organisations that are working for change in Burma through an array or programmes, workshops and trainings. (Photo: Sander)**

The recent unprecedented budget cuts have left ethnic populations and organisations on the border with less and less help from the international community. As a consequence, countless of organisations have recently been forced to discontinue their projects. In many places, people now lack food and medicine because aid organisations have cut their funding. CBOs along Burma's borders have said that it is too early to cut humanitarian aid as ethnic ceasefires remain unstable and there is not yet genuine peace in border areas (Karen News, June, 2013, May 2014; Lawi Weng, February, 2012).

It should also be taken into consideration that while some positive developments are taking place, many repressive laws have not been changed, vast majority of people are living in poverty, and there is still a great need for schools and hospitals, especially in border areas. The international donor community should also keep in mind that organisations working out of Rangoon not only have to work in cooperation with the Burmese government but they simply do not have access to most areas where cross-border aid has been operating. Furthermore, as these organisations extend their access further into ethnic regions, they bring more Burma Army troops with them, thus counteracting the benefits of their assistance (Kevin Malseen in Saw Yan Naing, May, 2012). When aid is cut to refugees, who are forced to be dependent on outside aid, they feel forced to return to areas in Burma that are not yet safe, or live illegally outside the camps in Thailand with no protection.

The recent hype about international donors moving inside the country is seen as counterproductive by many actors who have developed a deep understanding of the situation. Many of the most vulnerable people such as refugees and IDPs as well as the government-critical movement can still be best reached and supported through aid that is not channelled inside. Pouring millions of dollars inside the country is too often helping the government, not the people, become stronger, thus potentially exacerbating the conflict rather than helping to bring about a solution. Donors and NGOs should keep in mind that the government of Burma does not represent the people and is not working for them.

For many people of Burma along the Thailand-Burma border the only changes due to the recent reforms are exclusion and growing fear and uncertainty amidst reduced aid and rumours of forced repatriation. If we wish to see genuine transformation toward a democratic and just society for all peoples of Burma, it is imperative that the myriad organisations and vulnerable ethnic populations on the Thailand-Burma border are included in the democratisation and national reconciliation process, and that aid is continued until genuine and sustainable peace is achieved.

## Recent Talks of Repatriation

The recent political changes and ceasefires in Burma have resulted in widespread and grossly premature talks of refugee repatriation. Although the consensus is that conditions are not yet conducive for refugees to return, there are now significant concerns that refugee camps on the Thailand-Burma border could be closed and refugees repatriated before they can do so with a sense of dignity and hope.

*"Our main need is security. We want the Burmese soldiers out of our area, and take the landmines they planted out too. When we return, we don't want the Burmese soldiers harassing us again." (Karen man, CIDKP focus group, Palaw Township, interviewed in June 2008; TBC, 2008, p. 14)*

Talks about repatriation coupled with reduced aid have caused anxiety among the camp communities as most refugees do not feel safe returning to their homeland. Thailand has issued repeated threats to send refugees back to Burma (see e.g. Saw Yan Naing, September, 2012) and to close down the camps (Chitradon, April 2011; Saw Yan Naing, July, 2014b). This is a significant concern as formidable obstacles for safe repatriation, including the ongoing human rights violations in ethnic border areas as well as widespread landmine contamination, still remain, and genuine and lasting peace is yet nowhere in sight.

It is also worrying that both Thai authorities and the UNHCR have forcibly returned refugees back to Burma in the past despite grave ongoing human rights violations. In 1995, UNHCR "voluntarily" repatriated over 200,000 Burmese refugees from Bangladesh, most of them Rohingya. In 1996, at least 10,000 refugees attempted a desperate return to Bangladesh where the UNHCR was now denied any operational role. At least 15 women and young children drowned to death. As pointed out by the Human Rights Watch (1996); "The 1996 exodus from Burma raises several important questions about the UNHCR's repatriation operation from Bangladesh and about the promotion of 'voluntary' return to countries with particularly abusive governments." The UNHCR also acknowledged the issue:

*"…in some instances UNHCR has placed too much emphasis on early return to countries of origin which has resulted in return movements to less than favourable*

*conditions." (UNHCR, Oslo Declaration and Plan of Action, June 1994, as cited in Human Rights Watch, 1996).*

According to the Arakanese National Rohingya Organisation (ARNO), many more refugees also lost their lives over the years whilst resisting forced repatriation from Bangladesh to Burma (ARNO, 2012).

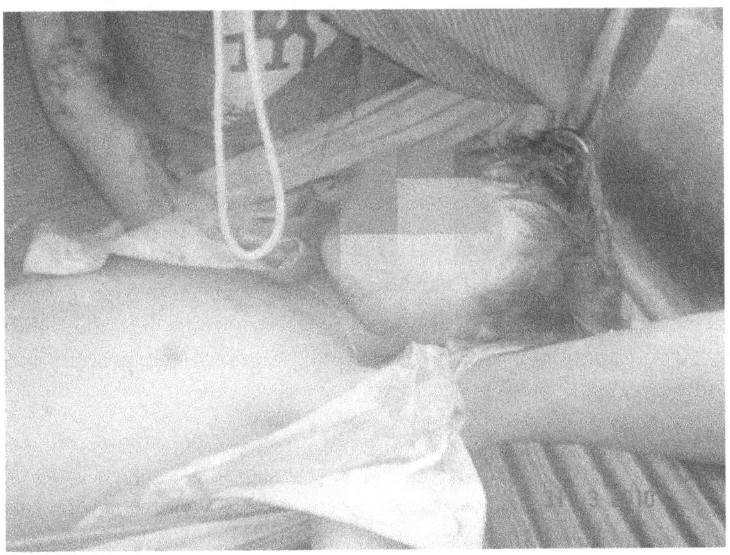

**A 10-year-old boy injured by an unexploded M7 cartridge after being forcibly repatriated to Burma in 2010. (Photo: KHRG)**

In 1996, Thailand forced Mon refugees near Sangkhlaburi to go back to Burma following a ceasefire signed between the New Mon State party (NMSP) and the Burmese government. After been forcibly repatriated, these Mon refugees remained far from their original homeland, received inadequate aid, and were unable to support themselves, according to the TBC (2004). The ceasefire did not lead to political dialogue, as none of them have, and subsequently broke in 2010. A new ceasefire was signed again 2012, but similarly to all the numerous ceasefires signed between the government and ethnic armies since the 1990s, the government has made no indication of actually discussing the possibility of establishing a federal union. As long as the government refuses to discuss the political goals of the ethnic organisations, all ceasefires are bound to be broken.

Thousands are now holding their breath praying that the past mistakes by the UNHCR and the Thai government will not be repeated in the Karen and Karenni camps on the Thailand-Burma border. Despite the positive change that has emerged under the Thein Sein administration, much more needs to be done before lasting peace and security can become a reality. Repatriation should arguably be a refugee-led voluntary operation and not enforced by outside actors.

*"I don't think you really need to return refugees back because if conditions were right, the refugees would go back of their own free will." (Aung San Suu Kyi on June 2, 2012; Burma Partnership short documentary "Nothing About Us Without Us" highlighting refugees' voices about repatriation from camps along the Thailand border back into Burma)*

Furthermore, there are also significant concerns that refugees and local CBOs have been left out of the repatriation planning. The key to successful return will not only be that it is voluntary but also that community participation is guaranteed in all stages of the preparation and planning process.

*"The refugees and internally displaced people are part of the solution, not the problem, and we all pray that before long they will be able to go back to Burma/Myanmar and play an important role in helping build a modern and peaceful nation." (Jack Dunford, Executive Director of TBC 1984-2012; TBC, 2013a)*

On their website, the UNHCR (2013) listed as one of their targets and objectives for 2013 in Thailand that, "All persons of concern in the nine camps have access to information on conditions in potential return areas in Myanmar (Burma) and on basic protection standards regarding voluntary repatriation." At the same time, there seemed to be no public information on where the refugees would go and refugees themselves seemed utterly unaware of anything related to the repatriation planning (based on Burma Link's interviews with refugees in September 2012, March 2013, November 2013, December 2014, and January 2015). The situation seems largely the same today, and by January 2015, the UNHCR had removed this target from their website (UNHCR, 2015).

In March 2013, the KRC issued a statement outlining ten points to repatriation, including a nationwide ceasefire, settling of political conflicts, and respect for universal human rights (Karen News, March,

2013). The KRC said again in May 2013 that it wants refugees to return only after the building of a genuine peace between the government and the KNU, and that when it is time to implement repatriation, all refugees should be returned at the same time and not as part of a "repatriation pilot" as suggested by the Burmese government (Saw Khar Su Nyar, May, 2013).

In May and June 2013, refugees' fears of premature repatriation were fuelled following a UN-led profiling survey. More than 3,600 refugees in Mae La camp signed a petition refusing to participate in the survey, claiming the questionnaire solicited answers that favour repatriation (Sullivan, June, 2013). The refugees feared that the information could be used as an indication of "voluntary return" and demanded that the survey be re-authored with their participation and approval. With help from Burma Link, the petition was delivered to the UNHCR and an article about the issue was published on the Democratic Voice of Burma (see Sullivan, June, 2013). Although the survey never got refugees' approval, it saw some important changes; refugees now needed to rank a preference of minimum two options for their future, instead of three (which meant they no longer had to indicate that going back to Burma is one of the choices they voluntarily chose for their future). The profiling survey has now been conducted in all nine camps along the border.

Refugees still remained skeptical about the underlying motives of the survey and the fact that it was conducted with tablets. One young refugee woman, Christine, told Burma Link in May 2014 that "even though we say the real answer, they [Mae Fa Luang Foundation, a Thai NGO that was subcontracted to conduct the survey] can change it later by themselves (Burma Link, 2014b)."

After the Thai military took over power in a coup in May, 2014, refugees' concerns and fears have grown even more. The junta has significantly restricted refugees' movement, announced that all refugees will be repatriated in 2015, and conducted a head count in the camps (see e.g. Saw Yan Naing, July, 2014a, 2014b). Thai authorities have given very little details of their repatriation plans or the underlying reasons for the head count. The UNHCR has also recently started their own headcount in the camps, which most refugees think will give them a chance to register as refugees and be resettled. Although the UNHCR has announced that the headcount is not an official registration, the refugees have little faith in the organisation telling them the truth; most think this is their last chance to get out and start a new life.

*"We don't know when they will close the camp, or when they close the camp, where we should go. We don't know… if authorities arrange forced repatriation, refugees will refuse to go back and it can build tension between refugees and authorities." (Christine, 22, Karen refugee, spoke with Burma Link in Mae La refugee camp in May 2014; Burma Link, 2014b)*

Currently none of the original reasons why refugees fled have been sustainably resolved, and it is imperative that the refugees are not forced, directly or indirectly, to go back to the country that they so desperately escaped from.

**There are still 110,000 refugees in the Thailand-Burma border camps. (Photo: Burma Link)**

## References


AAPP (2011). *AAPP 2011 Annual Report.* Assistance Association for Political Prisoners (Burma). www.aappb.org/AAPP_2011_ANNUAL_REPORT.pdf. Accessed September 10, 2012.

ARNO (2012). *Plight of the Rohingya: Solution?* Arakan Rohingya National Organisation, September 30, 2012. http://www.burmalibrary.org/docs14/THE_PLIGHT_OF_ROHINGYA-SOLUTION-Rev.pdf. Accessed October 10, 2012.

Bangkok Post (May, 2012). *As Myanmar opens, donor exit at border puts dreams in peril.* Bangkok Post [online], May 20, 2012, http://www.bangkokpost.com/news/investigation/294235/as-myanmar-opens-donor-exit-at-border-puts-dreams-in-peril. Accessed August 15, 2012.

Booth, A. (2003). *The Burma Development Disaster in Comparative Historical Perspective.* SOAS Bulletin of Burma Research 1(1), pp. 1-23.

Burma Link (2014a). *'I want peace, I really want it to be true'.* Story of Noe Myint, published on Burma Link's website on February 26, 2014. Available at http://www.burmalink.org/want-peace-really-want-true/

Burma Link (2014b). *'Authorities Should Take Action for Refugees NOW': Young Refugee Woman.* Interview with Christine, published on Burma Link's website on June 21, 2014. Available at http://www.burmalink.org/authorities-take-action-refugees-now-young-refugee-woman/.

Burma Partnership (2012). *Nothing About Us Without Us: Refugees' Voices About their Return to Burma.* A short documentary by Burma Partnership. Filmed and Directed by Timothy Syrota. Available at https://www.youtube.com/watch?v=gOW07BsBdrM.

Chitradon, B. (April, 2011). *Thailand wants to close Myanmar refugee camps.* AFP [online], April 11, 2011. http://reliefweb.int/report/myanmar/thailand-wants-close-myanmar-refugee-camps. Accessed February 18, 2015.

*COERR – Project.* http://www.coerr.org/Eng/project.html

Davis, B., Gittleman, A., Sollom, R., Richards, A., & Beyrer, C. (2012). *Bitter Wounds and Lost Dreams: Human Rights under Assault in Karen State, Burma.* Physicians for Human Rights (PHR), August, 2012. http://physiciansforhumanrights.org/library/reports/bitter-wounds-and-lost-dreams.html. Accessed September 1, 2012. © 2012 by Physicians for Human Rights.

Government of Burma (2003). *The Rights of the Child Consideration of Reports Submitted by States Parties under Article 44 of the Convention, Second periodic reports of States parties due in 1998, Myanmar.* State Party Report, November 5, 2003. http://tb.ohchr.org/default.aspx?Symbol=CRC/C/70/Add.21. Accessed September 5, 2012.

Green-Rauenhorst, M., Jacobsen, K., & Pyne, S. (2008). *Invisible in Thailand. Documenting the Need for International Protection for Burmese.* International Rescue Committee. https://wikis.uit.tufts.edu/confluence/download/attachments/14553674/Invisible_longerVersion_withCover.pdf?version=1. Accessed August 10, 2012.

Human Rights Watch (1996). *Burma: The Rohingya Muslims: Ending a Cycle of Exodus?* Human Rights Watch report, September 1996. http://www.hrw.org/legacy/summaries/s.burma969.html. Accessed February 18, 2015. © 1996 by Human Rights Watch

Human Rights Watch (2007). *Sold to be Soldiers. The Recruitment and Use of Child Soldiers in Burma.* Human Rights Watch report, October 2007. www.hrw.org/reports/2007/burma1007/burma1007webwcover.pdf. Accessed December 19, 2013. © 2007 by Human Rights Watch

Human Rights Watch (2010). *From the Tiger to the Crocodile: Abuse of Migrant Workers in Thailand.* Human Rights Watch report, February 2010. http://www.hrw.org/reports/2010/02/23/tiger-crocodile. Accessed November 20, 2010. © 2010 by Human Rights Watch.

Human Rights Watch (2012a). *Country Summary: Burma.* Human Rights Watch report, January 2012. http://www.hrw.org/sites/default/files/related_material/burma_2012.pdf.pdf. Accessed February 18, 2015. © 2012 by Human Rights Watch.

Human Rights Watch (2012b). *Ad Hoc and Inadequate. Thailand's Treatment of Refugees and Asylum Seekers*. Human Rights Watch report, September 2012. http://www.hrw.org/sites/default/files/reports/thailand0912.pdf. Accessed February 18, 2015. © 2012 by Human Rights Watch.

IDMC (2014). *Myanmar IDP Figure Analysis*. Internal Displacement Monitoring Centre. http://www.internal-displacement.org/south-and-south-east-asia/myanmar/figures-analysis. Accessed February 16, 2015.

Karen News (February, 2012). *BREAKING NEWS: Fire at Umpiem Mai Refugee Camp destroys 1000 houses*. Karen News [online], February 23, 2012. http://karennews.org/2012/02/breaking-news-fire-at-umpiem-mai-refugee-camp-destroys-1000-houses.html/. Accessed November 7, 2014.

Karen News (March, 2013). *Karen Refugees Committee's 10 Points to Repatriation*. Karen News [online], March 26, 2013. http://karennews.org/2013/03/karen-refugees-committees-10-points-to-repatriation.html/. Accessed December 23, 2013.

Karen News (June, 2013). *Karen Groups Concerned Cross-Border Humanitarian Aid Decreasing*. Karen News [online], June 3, 2013. http://karennews.org/2013/06/karen-groups-concerned-decreased-cross-border-humanitarian-aid.html/. Accessed December 23, 2013.

Karen News (November, 2013). *Australian Govt Cuts Dr Cynthia's Funding*. Karen News [online], November 6, 2013. http://karennews.org/2013/11/australian-govt-cuts-dr-cynthias-funding.html/. Accessed December 23, 2013.

Karen News (May, 2014). *Karen Women's Group Condemns Aid Cuts to Thai-Burma Border Refugees*. Karen News [online], May 28, 2014. http://karennews.org/2014/05/karen-womens-group-condemns-aid-cuts-to-thai-burma-border-refugees.html/. Accessed December 23, 2014.

KHRG (1995). *New Attacks on Karen Refugee Camps*. An Independent Report by the Karen Human Rights Group, May 5, 1995 / KHRG #95-16. http://www.khrg.org/khrg95/khrg9516.html. Accessed March 28, 2013.

KHRG (2008). *Growing up under Militarisation: Abuse and Agency of Children in Karen State*. Karen Human Rights Group, April 2008.

http://www.khrg.org/sites/default/files/khrg0801_3.pdf. Accessed December 19, 2013.

KHRG (2013). *Losing Ground: Land conflicts and collective action in eastern Myanmar.* Karen Human Rights Group, March 2013. http://www.khrg.org/khrg2013/LosingGroundKHRG-March2013-FullText.pdf. Accessed March 20, 2013.

KHRG (2014). *Truce or Transition? Trends in Human Rights Abuse and Local Response in Southeast Myanmar since the 2012 Ceasefire.* Report by Karen Human Rights Group (KHRG), May 2014. http://www.burmalink.org/wp-content/uploads/2014/05/khrg_-_truce_or_transition_-_english_briefer.pdf

La Guardia, A. (June, 2005). *Burma's 'slow genocide' is revealed through the eyes of its child victims.* The Telegraph [online], June 24, 2005. http://www.telegraph.co.uk/news/worldnews/asia/burmamyanmar/1492726/Burmas-slow-genocide-is-revealed-through-the-eyes-of-its-child-victims.html#. Accessed September 10, 2012.

Lawi Weng (February, 2012). *Kachin Peace Key to Mon Ceasefire.* The Irrawaddy [online], February 8, 2012. http://www2.irrawaddy.org/article.php?art_id=22997&Submit=Submit. Accessed August 25, 2012.

Lawi Weng (April, 2012). *CBOs Suffer Lack of Funds in Post-Election Burma.* The Irrawaddy [online], April 27, 2012. http://www.irrawaddy.org/archives/3245. Accessed August 25, 2012.

Mizzima (October, 2012). *UN official calls for plan to repatriate Burmese refugees.* Mizzima [online], October 25, 2012. http://www.mizzima.com/news/regional/8288-un-official-calls-for-planning-to-repatriate-burmese-refugees.html. Accessed October 28, 2012.

Naw Noreen (July, 2013). *Migrant Schools Face Closure Amid Funding Cuts.* DVB [online], July 12, 2013. http://www.dvb.no/news/migrant-schools-face-closure-amid-funding-cuts/29659. Accessed December 23, 2013.

ND-Burma (2012a). *Extreme Measures: Torture and Ill Treatment in Burma since the 2010 Elections.* Network for Human Rights Documentation – Burma report, May 2012. http://www.nd-burma.org/reports/item/94-

extreme-measures-torture-and-ill-treatment-in-burma-since-the-2010-elections.html. Accessed August 23, 2012.

ND-Burma (2012b). *Report on the Human Rights Situation in Burma. April-September 2012.* Network for Human Rights Documentation – Burma report. http://www.nd-burma.org/reports/item/download/97.html. Accessed September 1, 2012.

ND-Burma (2013). *Report on the Human Rights Situation in Burma January to June 2013.* www.burmalink.org/wp-content/uploads/2013/10/ND-Burma.Burmese.Human-rights-violations-in-Burma-Jan-Jun-2013.pdf.

ND-Burma (2014a). *Report on the Human Rights Situation in Burma. January – June 2014.* Network for Human Rights Documentation – Burma report. http://nd-burma.org/?wpdmact=process&did=NDIuaG90bGluaw. Accessed October 10, 2014.

ND-Burma (2014b). *Report on the Human Rights Situation in Burma (July – December 2013).* Network for Human Rights Documentation – Burma report. http://nd-burma.org/?wpdmact=process&did=MzAuaG90bGluaw. Accessed October 24, 2014.

Poe Kwa Lay (November, 2012). *Two Mae La camp refugees shot and killed.* Karen News [online], November 12, 2012. http://karennews.org/2012/11/two-mae-la-camp-refugees-shot-and-killed.html/. Accessed December 16, 2014.

RFA (March, 2013). *Burma's Military Rejects Rights Abuse Charges.* Radio Free Asia [online], March 27, 2013. http://www.rfa.org/english/news/burma/military-03272013175507.html. Accessed March 29, 2013.

Rogers, B. (2004). *A Land Without Evil. Stopping the Genocide of Burma's Karen People.* Oxford: Monarch Books.

Refugees International (2012). *Burma.* http://refugeesinternational.org/where-we-work/asia/burma. Accessed September 1, 2012.

Refugees International (2014). *Myanmar.* refugeesinternational.org/where-we-work/asia/myanmar. Accessed November 7, 2014.

Saw Khar Su Nyar (April, 2013). *DKBA and Govt militia fighting kills one and wounds one.* Karen News [online], April 30, 2013. http://karennews.org/2013/04/dkba-and-govt-militia-fighting-kills-one-and-wounds-one.html/. Accessed May 15, 2013.

Saw Khar Su Nyar (May, 2013). *Refugees wary of Govt repatriation 'pilot'.* Karen News [online], May 2, 2013. http://karennews.org/2013/05/refugees-wary-of-govt-repatriation-pilot.html/. Accessed May 15, 2013.

Saw Yan Naing (May, 2012). *As Donors Go into Burma, Cross-border Aid Dries Up.* The Irrawaddy [online], May 15, 2012. http://www.irrawaddy.org/archives/4232. Accessed March 25, 2013.

Saw Yan Naing (September, 2012). *Refugees Could Go Back Within One Year: Thailand.* The Irrawaddy [online], September 14, 2012. http://www.irrawaddy.org/archives/14013. Accessed October, 5, 2012.

Saw Yan Naing (July, 2014a). *Travel Restrictions Tighten for Burmese Refugees in Thailand.* The Irrawaddy [online], July 2, 2014. Available at http://www.burmalink.org/travel-restrictions-tighten-burmese-refugees-thailand/

Saw Yan Naing (July, 2014b). *Uncertainty, Concern Surround Thai Govt Headcount of Refugees.* The Irrawaddy [online], July 30, 2014.http://www.irrawaddy.org/burma/uncertainty-concern-surround-thai-govt-headcount-refugees.html. Accessed November 7, 2014.

Saw Yan Naing (September, 2014). *More Clashes Between Govt and Karen Rebels in Mon State.* The Irrawaddy [online], September 29, 2014. http://www.irrawaddy.org/burma/clashes-govt-karen-rebels-mon-state.html. Accessed October 10, 2014.

Shan Herald (September, 2012). *Ceasefire only "with government, not with army".* Shan Herald [online], September 11, 2012. http://www.english.panglong.org/index.php?option=com_content&view=article&id=4935:ceasefire-only-with-government-not-with-army&catid=86:war&Itemid=284. Accessed October 10, 2012.

SHRF & SWAN (2002*). License to rape. The Burmese military regime's use of sexual violence in the ongoing war in Shan State.* A joint report by The Shan Human Rights Foundation & The Shan Women's Action Network,

May 2012. http://burmalink.org/wp-content/uploads/2014/01/Licence_Rape_english.pdf

South, A. (2011). *Burma's Longest Running War: Anatomy of the Karen Conflict.* Transnational Institute (TNI) & Burma Center Netherlands (BCN). http://www.shanland.org/index.php?option=com_content&view=article&id=3548:burmas-longest-war-anatomy-of-the-karen-conflict&catid=mailbox&Itemid=279. Accessed September 25, 2012.

South, A., Perhult, M., & Carstensen, N. (2010). *Conflict and Survival: self-protection in south-east Myanmar.* Chatham House/Royal Institute of International Affairs.

S'Phan Shaung (August, 2014). *Migrant Schools Struggle To Keep Going As International Funders Pull Out.* Karen News [online], August 28, 2014. http://karennews.org/2014/08/migrant-schools-struggle-to-keep-going-as-international-funders-pull-out.html/. Accessed September 20, 2014.

Sullivan, F. (June, 2013). *Fearing Repatriation, Mae La Refugees Shun Profiling Survey.* DVB [online], June 5, 2013. http://www.dvb.no/news/fearing-repatriation-mae-la-refugees-shun-profiling-survey/28656. Accessed December 23, 2013.

TBC (2004). *Between worlds: Twenty years on the border.* The Border Consortium. Available at http://www.burmalink.org/wp-content/uploads/2013/12/TBC-2004.-Between-worlds_Twenty-years-on-the-border1.pdf

TBC (2008). *Internal Displacement and International Law in Eastern Burma.* The Border Consortium. www.tbbc.org/idps/report-2008-idp-english.pdf. Accessed December 19, 2013.

TBC (2011). *Displacement and Poverty in Southeast Burma/Myanmar.* The Border Consortium. http://www.tbbc.org/idps/report-2011-idp-en.zip. Accessed August 15, 2012.

TBC (2012a). *Programme Report 2012 January to June.* The Border Consortium. http://www.tbbc.org/resources/2012-6-mth-rpt-jan-jun.zip. Accessed October 10, 2012.

TBC (2012b). *Changing Realities, Poverty and Displacement in South East Burma/Myanmar – 2012 Survey.*

http://theborderconsortium.org/idps/report-2012-idp-en.zip. Accessed December 19, 2013

TBC (2013a). *Programme Report July to December 2012.* The Border Consortium. http://theborderconsortium.org/resources/2012-6-mth-rpt-jul-dec.zip. Accessed March 26, 2013.

TBC (2013b). *Programme Report January to June 2013.* The Border Consortium. http://theborderconsortium.org/resources/2013-6-mth-rpt-jan-jun.zip. Accessed December 18, 2013.

TBC (2013c). *Poverty, Displacement and Local Governance in South East Burma/Myanmar – 2013 Survey.* The Border Consortium, November 2013. http://burmalink.org/wp-content/uploads/2013/12/report-2013-idp-en-tbc.pdf

TBC (September, 2013). *Rice Rations Being Changed for Refugees from Burma/Myanmar in November.* The Border Consortium Press Release, September 18, 2013.
http://www.theborderconsortium.org/announcements/2013-09-18-news-ration-changed.pdf. Accessed December 23, 2103.

TBC (2014a). *Programme Report January – June 2014.* The Border Consortium.
http://www.theborderconsortium.org/media/51534/2014-6-Mth-Rpt-Jan-Jun.pdf. Accessed October 10, 2014.

TBC (2014b). *Protection and Security Concerns in Southeast Burma/Myanmar.* The Border Consortium, November 2014.
http://www.theborderconsortium.org/media/54376/report-2014-idp-en.pdf. Accessed February 19, 2015.

TBC (December, 2014). *Refugee and IDP Camp Populations: December 2014.* The Border Consortium.
http://www.theborderconsortium.org/media/56063/2014-12-dec-map-tbc-unhcr.pdf. Accessed February 18, 2015.

The Human Rights Center & the Center for Public Health and Human Rights (2007). *The Gathering Storm: Infectious Diseases and Human Rights in Burma.* http://www.soros.org/sites/default/files/storm_20070709.pdf. Accessed August 10, 2012.

UN General Assembly (2014a). *Resolution adopted by the General Assembly on 27 December 2013.*

http://www.altsean.org/Docs/UNGA%20Resolutions/Res%2068%20242.pdf. Accessed October 27, 2014.

UNHCR (2010). *United Nations Convention Relating to the Status of Refugees.* www.unhcr.org/3b66c2aa10.html. Accessed August 20, 2012.

UNHCR (2012). *2012 UNHCR country operations profile – Thailand.* http://www.unhcr.org/pages/49e489646.html.

UNHCR (2013). *2013 UNHCR country operations profile – Thailand.* http://www.unhcr.org/pages/49e489646.html. Accessed December 16, 2013.

UNHCR (2015a). *2015 UNHCR country operations profile – Thailand.* http://www.unhcr.org/pages/49e489646.html. Accessed February 16, 2015.

UNHCR (2015b). *2015 UNHCR country operations profile – Myanmar.* http://www.unhcr.org/pages/49e4877d6.html. Accessed February 16, 2015.

UN OCHA (2004). *The Guiding Principles on Internal Displacement.* The United Nations Publication. http://www.unhcr.org/43ce1cff2.html. Accessed March 28, 2013.

UN Office of the High Commissioner for Human Rights (July, 2014). *Statement of the Special Rapporteur on the Situation of Human Rights in Myanmar.* Published July 26, 2014. http://www.ohchr.org/EN/NewsEvents/Pages/DisplayNews.aspx?NewsID=14909&LangID=E. Accessed October 27, 2014.

U.S. Campaign for Burma (2012a). *Human Rights and Conflicts.* U.S. Campaign for Burma reports. http://uscampaignforburma.org/resources/reports/13-resources/67-human-rights-and-conflicts.html. Accessed September 1, 2012.

US State Department (2013). *Burma 2012 Human Rights Report.* http://www.state.gov/documents/organisation/204400.pdf. Accessed May 10, 2013.

US State Department (2014). *Burma 2013 Human Rights Report.* www.state.gov/documents/organisation/220394.pdf. Accessed October 10, 2014.

WLB (2011). *The Founding and Development of the Women's league of Burma.* Report by the Women's League of Burma. Available at http://www.burmalink.org/wp-content/uploads/2013/12/WLB-2011.-The-Founding-and-Development-of-the-Women%E2%80%99s-League-of-Burma_A-Herstory.pdf

www.ingramcontent.com/pod-product-compliance
Ingram Content Group UK Ltd.
Pitfield, Milton Keynes, MK11 3LW, UK
UKHW021654190726
13853UKWH00001B/252

9 789526 828305